MOM
COLORING BOOK

Get FREE printable coloring pages and discounted book prices sent straight to your inbox every week!

Sign up today at:

www.adultcoloringworld.net

WOO HOO IT'S FRIDAY!

OH WAIT I'M A MOM

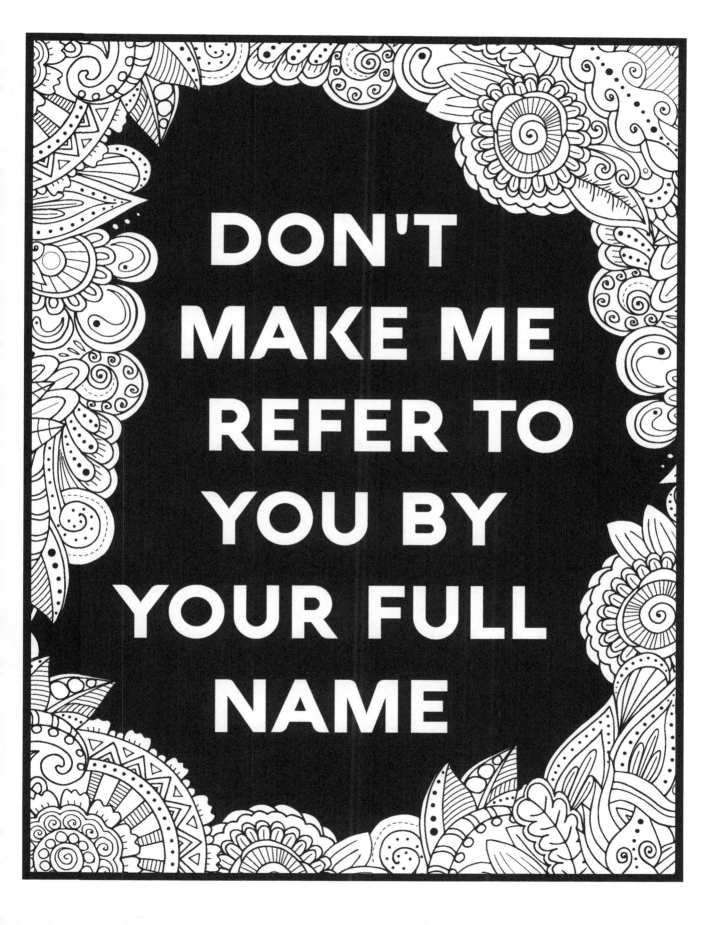

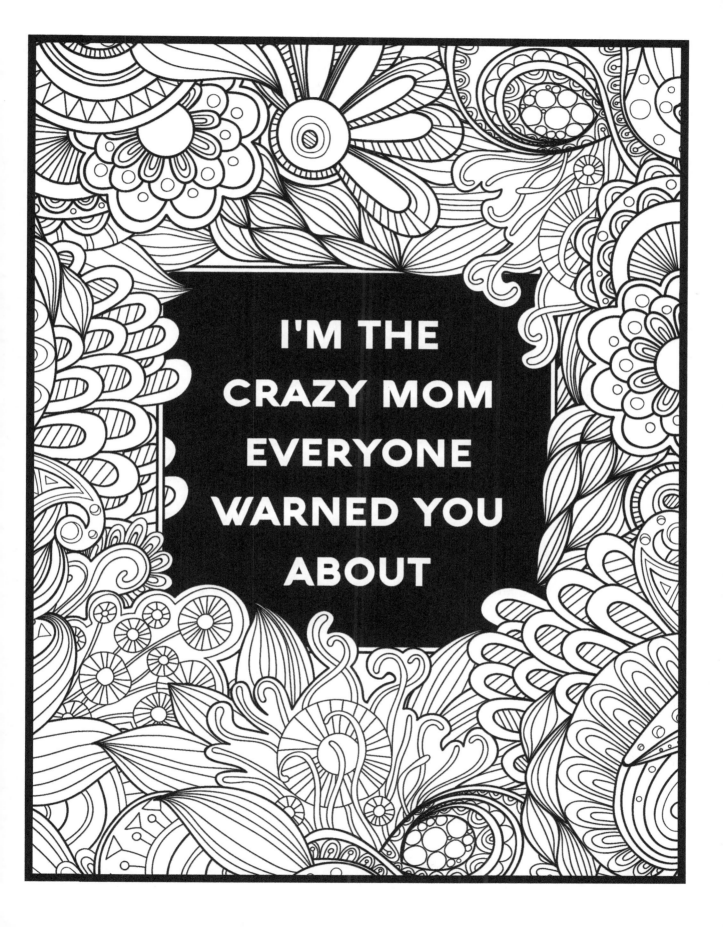

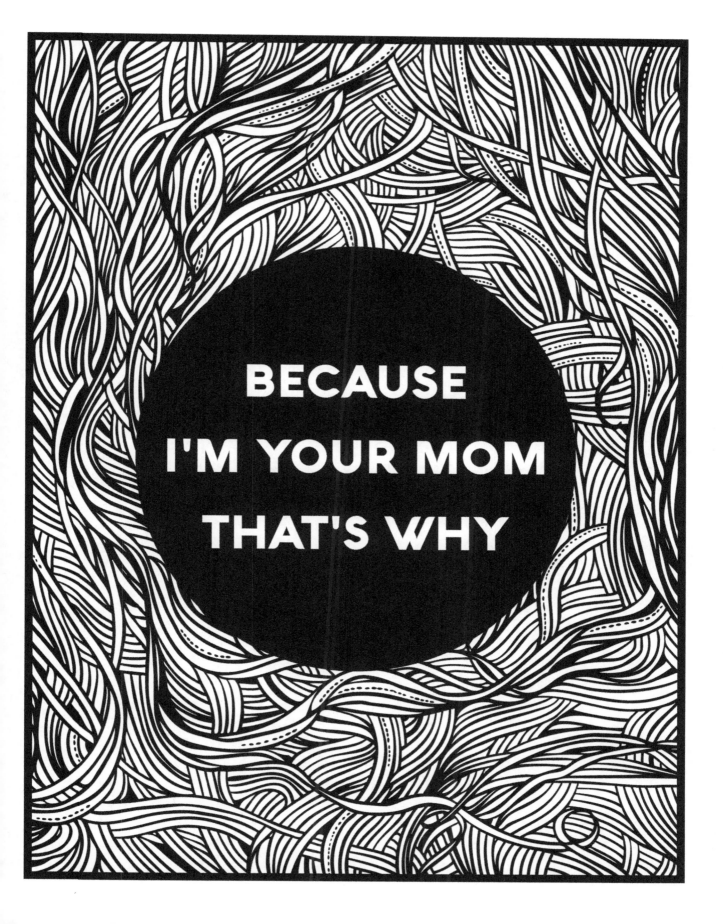

COLOR TEST PAGE

COLOR TEST PAGE

Made in the USA
Monee, IL
27 May 2022

97123126R00050